HOUSE WITHOUT A DREAMER

HOUSE WITHOUT A DREAMER

by Andrea Hollander Budy

For Mark
with deep gratitude for
helping this manuscript
become a book and for
gracing its cover with
your good words.
Thank you, thank
you. And for your
own fine poems, which
light the way.
Love
Andrea
December 93

STORY LINE PRESS

1993

Published by Story Line Press, Inc., Three Oaks Farm, Brownsville, OR 97327

This publication was made possible thanks in part to the generous support of the Nicholas Roerich Museum, the Andrew W. Mellon Foundation, and our individual contributors.

Library of Congress Cataloging-in-Publication Data

Budy, Andrea Hollander, 1947–
    House without a dreamer / by Andrea Hollander Budy.
        p.   cm.
    ISBN 0-934257-83-3 : $9.95
    I. Title.
PS3552.U349H681993
811'.54—dc20   93-31002
                                                    CIP

ACKNOWLEDGMENTS

The Albany Review, "Snow White"; *Birmingham Poetry Review,* "The Color of the Sky"; *The Chariton Review,* "Jack Sprat"; *Context South,* "Gretel"; *The Devil's Millhopper,* "One for the Money," "This Is Not a Letter But Another Poem"; *The Georgia Review,* "Advice," "Black," "Pigs," "When She Named Fire," "Women at Fifty"; *Half Tones to Jubilee,* "Trying to Explain"; *High Plains Literary Review,* "Fire," "This Is an Answer"; *Indiana Review,* "No One Wants to Be the Witch," "Asleep in the Forest"; *The Kenyon Review,* "Just"; *The Laurel Review,* "This Will Be My Only," "The Line"; *Nebraska Review,* "Because We Have Been Married a Long Time," "Trying to Understand What Isn't Said"; *Negative Capability,* Part III of "Trying to Explain"; *New England Review,* "What You Find"; *The Ohio Review,* "What I Want"; *The Pacific Review,* "Therapy"; *Plainsong,* Part I of "Trying to Explain" [as "Ghost"]; *Poetry,* "Firmly Married"; *Shenandoah,* "Choice"; *Slant,* "This," "The Old Woman Who Lived in a Shoe"; *Southern Poetry Review,* "Permission"; *Third Rail,* "Grief"; *Yarrow,* "Buttons," "Weeds," "When You Hear His Name"; *Zone 3,* "Dawn," "Poem for My Brother, Manager of a Go-go Bar in Roselle Park, New Jersey"

Some of these poems were included in the limited edition volumes *Living on the Cusp* (Moonsquilt Press, 1981), *Happily Ever After* (Panhandler Press of the University of West Florida, 1989), and *What the Other Eye Sees* (Wayland Press, 1991).

"Pigs" appeared in the 1985 edition of *Anthology of Magazine Verse and Yearbook of American Poetry* (Monitor Books), *The Georgia Review's* Fortieth Anniversary Poetry Retrospective issue (Fall 1986), and *Keener Sounds* (University of Georgia Press, 1987). "Poem for My Brother, Manager of a Go-go Bar in Roselle Park, New Jersey" won third prize in the 1990 Rainmaker Awards and an honorable mention in the 1991 *Pushcart Prize Anthology.*

The author is grateful to following people for their encouragement and support: Isabelle Budy, Jack Butler, Stephen Corey, Deborah Cummins, Geoffrey Douglas, Lola Haskins, Richard Hawley, Cynthia Kennedy, Gary Margolis, Phillip McMath, Alison Michel, Lee Potts, Loretta Price, Gary Schroeder, Terrell Tebbetts, Carol Thacker, Mark Wood, Virginia Wray, and the trustees, administration, staff, faculty, and students of Arkansas College.

Special thanks to David Jauss for his close reading of the manuscript, to Stanley W. Lindberg of *The Georgia Review* and Frank Steele of *Plainsong* for publishing my first poems, and to the Arkansas Arts Council and the National Endowment for the Arts for fellowships which provided time, encouragement, and much more.

for Todd and Brooke, who fill my house

and in memory of my mother,
Blanche Simon Hollander (1919-1970)

CONTENTS

WHEN SHE NAMED FIRE

it was a sound
she uttered, not a considered thing, nothing
her mind did. It was a sound
which burned her throat to come out
and announce itself for the thing
that was burning outside her
where the trees had been down
for years and which lit the sky
then disappeared and changed
to something black.

When she named the sun, she didn't think
of fire at all. *Sun*, she claimed,
because it was huge and unexplainable,
a oneness that she loved
for its ability to command
the whole sky and the earth, too;
and because it was the warmest thing
she knew, and she sang
its tunes and missed it every night.

She didn't name the moon at all. That was
the name it gave itself. At night she heard
it call. To her it was
another kind of sun, still white

but cold, an icy light
that narrows as it grows, that is not
light at all.

She thought she gave love's name
to love, that beating thing she could not
still. She might have called it
bird. Or *fire* again
for fire inside that gives no light
but burns and burns and does not
stop until she touches
what she loves, and then it only burns
again and makes her want
to name it something more.

THE COLOR OF THE SKY

No matter what I tell you about the sky tonight,
even if I tell you everything I know
about its dark rich blue, faded here
and there like the velvet jacket my mother
used to wear, and how much I loved her
when she wore it, how much I loved to touch
her arm or think about touching it, how sometimes
I would even walk deep into the walk-in closet,
dark as the sky is tonight, and reach
and find it by touch, and know it, electrically,
the way I know your body in our bed at night,
in the black room of that room, way in the back
where no one could find me, in the blue
black night of that soft cave, and the smell of it,
the faded smell of my mother there and the way
I felt—all velvet and alone and blue myself, and
somehow safe, just safe. No matter what I tell you
about the color of the sky tonight, you will not know
enough about the sky at all, about its magnificent blue
that I know I could touch, that changes and disappears
no matter how much I say, no matter how much
I want it to stay.

BEGINNING AND ENDING
WITH LINES FROM SHAKESPEARE

Whoever made us believe that all the world's a stage
must have known we'd drive as slowly as the car would go
past the aftermath of the accident, one young man holding
another man's head above the reddened pavement,

a woman still in the passenger seat holding her shoulder,
another, her hair in pink plastic curlers, pacing
that brief space between the cars, her eyes crazy,
her little boy in her arms, her girl trying to slow her

down. Whoever made us believe must have known
we would save that scene, however brief, save
even the sky's cumulus relief of gray against gray against gray,
that, against our wills, we'd take it all home

and play it again when we were most alone,
waiting by a telephone in a hallway,
praying him home, praying that other day's images away,
not wanting to see anymore the quick white bone

jutting through the man's leg as he lay
with his head in the other man's arms, not wanting, over and over,
to hear that ambulance racing to save not only
him. We believe we are more important than they,

that this cannot really happen to us. This is a game, we insist,
the next car we hear will be his pulling in,
this is only a stage
and all the men and women merely players.

PIGS

It is not the wolf
but his howl in the hollow wind

they fear. His mouth is a great cave
and that howl the master of it—

that sound calling like the night,
calling what is dark to its vacant center.

Straw by straw, stick by stick,
brick by solid brick, there is no way

to keep that sound from entering.
But try. Move in together, give birth,

have other kinds of dreams. Sleep
with a light turned on, with cotton in your ears.

And by the evening fire tell the stories
of your ancestors. Tell how clever they were,

how they tempted the Devil from the skins
of the innocent. How they burned Him

from those useless lives: Catholics, Jews,
witches, saints. And with fire like this.

With fire like this.

FIRE

The house was not touched.
But the trees are charred, our yard
is black, the grasses bladeless.
Everything we own looks different
now. Even knickknacks seem to have more
weight, the walls have grown, the furniture
replaced with replicas. And our son

does not want to go to bed.
What if it happens again
in my sleep, he does not ask,
but says. I sleep

much lighter now myself.
Weeks later I am up at 3 AM
to look at him, his face so perfect in
the moonlight. There's so little we can
count on. He's nearly nine. He nearly died
when he was born. And now we've come
this far. I see he's got the corner
of the blanket in his fist.
I want just this: to watch him
breathe all night, learn everything,
everything he is.

WEEDS

The last time I saw my mother
alive, I remember driving the familiar
miles to the hospital, sensing that this
might be the last time, and suddenly seeing
everything as if I'd never see it again:
houses, yards, fences, trees, weeds that
grew up along the edge of one driveway where
I waited for a light. It had been weeks
this time, and now she'd stopped eating.
There were dandelions on the hospital grounds
and crabgrass and pigweed. I remembered
the necklace she showed me how to make once
from dandelion flowers. The clouds made
shadows on the walkway. The elevator
smelled like medicine and powder.
In the bed my mother slept. Her breath
was uneven, and I wondered if she dreamed.
The room was filled with greenhouse
flowers. I wore that necklace for hours,
until it grew too limp to keep.

CHOICE

Whatever the truth is, I remember it
this way: the two of them arguing
over a dress, which one would be
the *right* dress, Ruth insisting
the flowered one my mother'd worn
to parties, Helen, whose face
by now was dark, her voice nasty,
accusing any choice that wasn't black
of blasphemy, disgusted anyone would even
think *that* dress. And then they looked
to me, her only daughter, after all, now
twenty-four and older than I'd ever be
again, and wanted me to arbitrate.
I'd be a traitor, whatever I said.
So I looked at them a long while,
nothing in my head but the picture
of my mother's face that morning
with finally a little peace in it again,
her body in the hospital bed,
the last bed, the last
face she'd ever have
for me. What did it matter
what they would dress her in
tomorrow, that day that only I
would always see? *Naked,* I thought,

the way she came. And then
I turned from the darkness
and the flowers, which were
the same, and from the two
of them in their overwhelming
grief which had taken them to this
tiniest of places, and what I thought
I said.

GRIEF

*The most terrible part of a great sorrow is not
the beginning, when the shock of grief throws one
into a state of exaltation which is almost anaesthetic
in its effects, but afterwards, long afterwards, when
people say, "Oh she has gotten over it."*
—Isadora Duncan

It is the cave you visit
in your dream. There are
no stars, no moon; and so
you swim naked, knowing
you cannot be seen.
You move down, down
through the black water,
and there is no end.
You see nothing, feel
only small waves passing
through your ears
as you descend.
It is not different
from other caves
in other dreams:
a secret place,
and you have learned
to breathe in it.

WHEN YOU HEAR HIS NAME

unexpectedly,
long after you have claimed

it wouldn't mean anything, you know
you have found the one name

you can never say,
never even bear to hear

even if it is now someone else's name,
a neighbor's child

and his mother snapping it at him
like a whip.

You try to make that sound just
a white sheet

the wind slaps
on the taut line. But you become

that line
holding everything above

the earth, stretched
house to post and back

again to house. Or you are
the post, placed

only to hold
the laundry up, keep

the line straight. You are not
the house, not a thing

someone can enter.

THE OLD WOMAN WHO LIVES IN A SHOE

She's only forty and she swears
they are not all hers.
She tells the man just passing through
she's not old enough
and laughs. Glasses clink.
The shoe doesn't fit.
Splash it down.
He does not ask whose.

> Should have crushed them,
> one by one, when they were pebbles.
> Should have been a baker's wife.
> Should have had another drink,
> not a dozen nights like this.
> Or mornings. She lifts
> the blankets to her chin
> as the gentleman leaves.

She's only thirty-three
and she believes he'll return.
The snow's buried the tulips twice since,
and someone new moves in that white room
again. But he gave his word, and she reads
the same psalm every night.

Should have passed them on
to someone else—that aunt
in Detroit. Or left.
Should have been a banker's wife.
Best part of church is the Eucharist.
She takes the lies with the wine
and pulls the blankets past her breasts
as another one leaves.

She's only twenty-five, twenty-three,
seventeen, and not naive, damn him.
The washing machine leaks
and the basement's flooded.
She stares at the bride on the cover
of the magazine, turns off
the TV and finds a mirror in it.
She ignores what she sees
and the walls thicken.

Should have stopped at two
and tried to recover. Should look
for the plunger and the sponge.
Should have been her father's wife.
She rubs the ashes from her head
as her husband comes.

She's only twelve.
She's only ten,
and she hates him even more when he leaves
her bed than when he's in it.
When she buttons her robe
there's someone else there,
and her mother stops speaking.

Should have left then, but she's afraid
for her sister. Should have confessed:
Hail Mary, full of blood,
the Lord's a sinner. Her dresses
won't fit. She hides what she dreads,
pulls up the sheets and pretends
she's dead.

WOMEN AT FIFTY

after Donald Justice

All of their doors
Have closed and their daughters'
Rooms betray a familiar faint perfume
That says *I'll not be back.*

They pause sometimes
At the top of the stairs
To stroke the bannister,
Its perfect knots.

They invite other women now
Only to clean. And like queens in fairy tales
They turn their heads from mirrors
That hold secrets they've kept

Even from themselves,
As they look into their husbands' faces
When their husbands say
They only look.

Women at fifty
Corner a cricket with a broom
And do not kill it, but shoo it out of the house
Into the abundant silence.

BUTTONS

Ivory, lucite, mother-of pearl, she sorts them
by kind and color and sews them on cards, files them
in drawers. The world's so large, even the storms
have names. It rains and the streets turn colors, too,
the hundred feet beneath those moving shades
all rushing somewhere else, so definite. But she
can be the center of a storm like this.
She's found a few in careless sidewalk cracks,
caught glimpses of some small perfectedness
and beelined through the moving, brooding crowd,
and, as if it were just some brush she must get through,
knelt down, a hazard now herself, and deftly as
a lioness whose pause and sigh can clean
a valley out, she's reached for one and calmly
picked it up. Her kitchen table, then, becomes
a lab. It lies so clean, so singular
and purposeful. What had reason once,
now, at least, has history. The world's
so deep, she lives on what floats up.

SOUP

At 4 PM, while her ex is sitting
in his easy chair somewhere in the gray
of his Iowa landscape, his desk high

with obligations, the unread
Sunday papers piled by his feet,
the winds faint, the traffic fainter,

the snowless cold out every
window of his house, and light
thrown through the clouds in such a way

there is no doubt what time
or day or state this is,
a little farther south

she will be standing at the kitchen sink
of her too familiar house, scraping
vegetables for soup and looking

out at the same bleak sky, trying
to remember how brilliant
the brittle trees have been,

listening to their fits
and twists in the wind, paring
carrot peels into the sink, then potato,

letting them pile there like spent
snake skins. If only he
would open this door, how warm

the afternoon would feel, how different
the falling of the light, how autumn,
not winter, the soup.

THERAPY

for James Twiggs

Years back when I thought
I needed that kind of listener,
I paid a therapist enough
to call her mine and sat
in her velvet chair an hour
each time and watched
that hour die and watched
her face and through her
window just behind I watched
the haze of Boston's sky
which was so alive
I thought it watched me back
as I spoke my mind
and it pulled clouds
across her frame from gray
to darker gray.

That kind of hour is like
a dream. And even now
I keep remembering
more the way she seemed
so like a cat
stretching, purring, preening
as she sat with her shoes

off and her legs curled up
and sometimes touched her
mouth and sometimes scratched
her brow. I remember that
more than anything she did
or did not say. She did not
save me. She may have
tried. I was lost
to time and men and, in my twenties
then, I kept mistaking time alone
for emptiness. And then one day
she fell asleep and even snored,
my voice a drone, the sky a storm.
Insulted, scared, cured? I guessed
that that was that. I tiptoed out
and took the streetcar home
and got a cat.

JACK SPRAT

If you'd known them at all
you'd never have called it

Perfect, heaven-made, or *fit*
as hand in glove. Convenient

perhaps, a habit perfected
in stride, mindlessly. To each

the other was the key
kept on the ring long after

it fits anything, a safe
familiar *clink* in the pocket.

At dinner neither spoke.
She picked over chicken bones,

licked her thick fingers, sometimes
laughed, and when he did not ask,

let it taper. He never asked.
Never made a sound when he ate

either. When she finished
she would listen for it. Not even

when he drank. And he never looked
inside her for any small versions

of either of them. To her
he seemed enough; though at night

the house echoed. Left alone
things should last. But whether

she chose Saint Mary, Therésa, or
Clare, and no matter how much weight

or how close she pressed the center
of it, their mattress never yielded

beside her, never even suggested
when or what he dreamt.

JUST

It was just a story, he said, emphasis
on *just* as if that were a diminishment,
an adjustment from third
into second and the hill to be
mounted, then the getting up it
in the appropriate gear. But the *just*
made no difference to her. It was
a story, perhaps, but she was
in it. She saw herself—the bitchy
one, the one whose hair is always
perfect, the one who screams more
than she speaks, who fixes the wrong
foods for company, who whimpers
over the dishes later but never cries
in front of anyone. Not even him,
though now, she thinks, he must have
known. Afterwards, she tries to be
the other woman, the one whose hair
was wild, who sang in the garden,
weeding. She tries to smile more, too,
and when she thinks she almost has it right
but isn't quite sure, she reads the story
again, finds out what else she can
become and then becomes it, just like that.

THE LINE

This is the side
on which my husband stays.
He stands long hours
in places like this, waiting
for me to run down, wear out,
discover my body again.

This is the other side,
the side on which strangers
beg. I go there daily
with butter and bread.
Sometimes I bake it.
I offer them rooms in our house,
an overstuffed chair, a porch swing,
a bed to sleep in.

Sometimes my husband wants
what the strangers get.
He goes for days
not eating, never getting rest.

He asks why I work so hard
and give away the cream,
why the best I earn

I never want to keep.
He says I have lost
exactly what I need.

He wants what I give
to be for him.

He draws the line
again and again,

and again I cross it.

FIRMLY MARRIED

is what he said but as he said it
swayed a little in my direction,
the hair on his neck so like
my son's, barely there, but golden
if you bothered looking.

He was looking at me anyway
no matter what he said,
a benefit of having spoken
his excuses so I'd excuse
anything he did thereafter.

I walked away.

And afterwards I thought
how easily he'd escaped
whatever I may have taken
from that look, that he wanted
it to be *my* invention, the way

I used to pull my stockings up
pretending not to notice Richie
watching, when I was nineteen
and wanted secretly my first time
to happen already, but wanted it

to be *his* doing, this undoing
I longed for desperately,
the way this man wants
some blameless ruin.

PERMISSION

When you have stood at the door
longer than two friends ought to,
one of your mates upstairs
tucking children in, the other
out of town; and when you stand
not gazing off into any distance
at all, recognizing that there
isn't any distance that wants
attention, except the three or four
inches between your face and his, that
that is the distance you'd like
permission to disclaim, erase, void,
you stop.

You step back, find something
simple and unnecessary to do
with your hands, hoping you won't
touch his arm or his face, hoping
he won't move any closer,
that he'll discover something
in the way, something that will
sway him somewhere else; or you hope
words will come, right words
that will shape what is necessary
to shape, so you can keep this
the way you want it: the wanting

and the stepping back. Not the finishing,
not that. As though the *right* words,
if you could find and say them, could really
save you, save you from saying what is
not right, like *yes* or *yes* or especially
the *yes* that is not spoken, which—with
or without permission—you seem already
to be saying nonetheless.

BLACK

Before his wife came back
I rose from his bed into the black
dress I'd brought, so stark a color
for early autumn, and buttoned it
all the way to my neck and said goodbye
and drove toward home. All day along that road

as I grew warm, I unbuttoned buttons one by one.
What little I have known of passion. It takes in
everything, seduces the most innocent.
Only road kills seemed to own that road: skunk, skunk,
armadillo, possum, possum, possum. Passion

travels in the dark—the animal
we do not truly know, the one
we never pet, the one so foreign
to our lives we do not have a sense
of what it eats or where it sleeps, and only know
its death. I meant

to watch the hills instead, the greens
reduced, the reds so dominant
the rest pull back.
My mother told me don't wear black until
you're grown. Back then I thought
of widow's clothes. The kind

of passion I have known
at first is wet and thunderous and new as grass
that's greener after rain, then briefly blazes red,
then is black and thunderous and wet—and then
the nakedness, the nakedness again.

NO ONE WANTS TO BE THE WITCH

no matter which story
this is. But today
in this story I'll play

the dark one, try on
her difficult clothing
that dazzles yet so easily

slips away. I'll sit
in the clearing and wait
for the boy to come with his simple

hunger and his single trick. If it's his tongue
he wishes to satisfy, I'll conjure the cinnamon
house. If it's love,

that chivalric game of bluff we play
to feed the animal the kind of power
it needs, I'll stay up

in the tower, fool him with my lonesome
melody and my long untangling. If it's fear
he wants, I'll give him thorny

messages to cut through and a little
blood. No matter who
I truly am, sorrow-filled

human, loneliest woman in love
only with him, I'll give him whatever
he's after, whatever he believes

he needs to see, be it princess
or virgin, whimpering
animal or mute, whatever

helplessness wants rescuing
and he both hero
and sword. But what will make him call me

witch, in the end, is how much of this
he will conjure for himself, how he will someday
know lust for what it was, love

for what it might or never
could have been. He'll be his own
witch then.

GRETEL

A woman is born to this:
sift, measure, mix, roll thin.

She learns the dough until
it folds into her skin and there is

no difference. Much later
she tries to lose it. Makes bets

with herself and wins enough
to keep trying. One day she begins

that long walk in unfamiliar woods.
She means to lose everything

she is. She empties her dark pockets,
dropping enough crumbs

to feed all the men who have ever
touched her or wished.

When she reaches the clearing
she is almost transparent—

so thin
the old woman in the house seizes

only the brother. You know the rest:
She won't escape that oven. She'll eat

the crumbs meant for him, remember
something of his touch, reach

for the sifter and the cup.

ASLEEP IN THE FOREST

after HANSEL & GRETTEL,
a painting by Monique Felix

They might have been lovers,
but lovers do not sleep

as close as this: stretched out
in the forest's sanctuary

as if God were about
instead of a witch.

Or else they sleep closer, hoping
closeness will be a kind of latch,

a madcap brace against the loneliness
they sense in happy endings.

They bend the story now and then,
remember the fox, the frog, the beauty

always hiding somewhere deeper than they've been.
Their sleep is innocent and blue

and they keep counting on togetherness
to take them in and bring them safely out.

They'd follow stars,
but stars don't penetrate this forest.

They follow lightning
bugs instead, as if the light itself

were all that mattered.
It's this mistake

that took them to the witch's house,
the first of many.

But not tonight.
Tonight they take their sleep

as we might step into a creek
together, and linger in it, let

what is bad
rise to the surface, unnoticed

for a moment, clouding the water,
then rinse itself away,

as we look only into
one another's eyes at what is good,

and know that that is all there is
and it will stay.

GETTING BACK

Thirteen days away, then three different planes
and the airport lounges between them,
the three hours north in the car
watching the white line blur toward home,
all the time wanting to see only
your eyes instead of the lights
of oncoming cars, wanting
your body back and the deep forgiving step
into that dark lake where we swim
toward the darkest part
waiting for light.
Wanting nothing else, taking
only what we believe we have to have
and finally reaching that limbo place
of not wanting, the wanting itself—
a plane so huge, so heavy you cannot believe
it will ever rise—having lifted with grace
and impossible ease.

THIS WILL BE MY ONLY

unfaithfulness.
I will take the man
you used to be and
remember him.
I will draw his lines
on your hands at night
while we lie awake
and speak to him
in dark places, even
while you sleep.
He will not leave me.
His turns will not be digressions,
nor will he place new feet on the sill
each day when he enters.
And his words will be few,
but I will know them the way
any woman knows the body
of her lover. I will hear them
every time we touch.

BECAUSE WE HAVE BEEN
MARRIED A LONG TIME

Tired after the meeting, he read
and I sat at my desk writing what I knew
I could not finish. Then we talked
a while in bed and made love as easily
as the moon moves through the constant
web of trees without getting caught.
That extraordinary, yet so common
we accept it without comment. Afterwards
we talked again, on into the starry night,
until I was so tired one star
seemed to be moving at my will.
I moved it with my eye.
But once I blinked it returned
to its corner of the window. High
on the power of the temporary
I played my game again and again,
all the time knowing that star
would win.

Tomorrow I want to rise early enough
to catch the first words steaming
off the earth, the sun just a chunk
of brilliant-colored rock

thrown out behind the treeline,
my thirst a runner's thirst,
and each deep breath I take
as new as a man's touch in a place
I've not been touched before.

ONE FOR THE MONEY

I would pay money to read a sex poem
in which the bodies don't SHINE.
                              —Frank Steele

In this one
they hesitate, lugging
the bedstead against the door first,
wiring some moth-balled blankets
to the tops of the windows,
pushing the stacks of cartons
out of the way.

The water is not yet on,
and she states some complaint,
all the time letting her clothes
dangle to the dark oak floor, naked
without its layers of flowered
linoleum or carpets. But the bed
is something they've shared
thirty years, and he coaxes her
onto it, pushing aside the pile
of linen and crumpled papers,
and her long unbraided hair,
her tame excuses.

They do not shine afterwards either,
though it is summer and the heat
in the room has risen even more.
It is just that there is no
eye to look in on them.
Outside that closed room
there is no one to imagine,
through that hole
in one hanging blanket,
whether a single shoot
of moonlight finds them
wet and still clinging
to the beginnings of things
again.

WHAT I WILL BE WHEN
I CANNOT BE WITH YOU

When the leaf turns
but does not fall, that will be me.
And when the leaf finally falls,
even if you are looking instead
at a flower, that, too, will be me.
And if the flower blooms, huge
and reckless, the soft yellow powder
inside that comes off on the legs
of a bee or on your finger or stains
the tip of your nose will be me,
as will the bud's seed that no one
sees when the bud fails to open,
and the vacant spot on the tree
that you see when you look again
and the leaf has dropped.

THIS IS NOT A LETTER
BUT ANOTHER POEM

Dear Loretta,
I've been doing what you said:
breaking out of bed before sunrise,
sitting at my desk before
my mind is set, watching
through the window as
again
the world is born.

But there are mornings
I can't help myself.
I don't want to be
the watcher anymore.
I'm tired of taking the pictures,
making the maps.
I leave my desk and step
out into darkness.
I want to be part of
the emptiness, part
of the unseeable landscape
that I sense is there,
a tree in the yard,
a mark on the curb.

When the sun comes up
I want to be
just a twig on the grass,
dew-covered and glistening,
standing as tall as a twig
can stand,
listening for wind
hoping for birds
or the hand of a child,
the mouth of a dog.

TRYING TO UNDERSTAND
WHAT ISN'T SAID

My mother still comes to me
in my sleep or late at night
if I've opened my eyes in the dark
of the dark, when the dead
still hover over us, whispering.

I don't hear that well anymore,
but her face is enough.
She looks as though she's on her way
to a party, skin perfect, eyes glistening.

It's that look she gave
when I was young
and she was on her way
someplace adult
without me, all dressed up,
and I wanted to go with her.
She did not say anything
but her look said, "Stay.
You'll have your turn later."

Out the window the stars
are plentiful. Day is still
a few hours away:
I have been so many places
and I don't know anything.

WHAT I WANT

When I've had enough of silence,
enough of its fog so thick this single
headlight I've become
beams out alone
into its soupy darkness,
suddenly I know
how lost I am.

This is the way
that longing always goes.
A stubborn light is shot in one
direction and does not go out, is not
returned. I want

to change this longing if I can.
I want to stop discounting
what I am. I want whatever's out there—
perhaps a word, perhaps a man—to part
that silence,

to clear the road ahead,
to signal dogs and rabbits,
to warn oncoming traffic
that someone mean and tired of longing
is speeding down this forlorn
road, careening fast past everything
she knows, top down,
radio blaring, leaning hard
on her persistent horn.

WHAT YOU FIND

for Alison Michel

. . . it is better
than gold, if you learn to accept what you find . . .
—William Stafford

It could be a racehorse, years later,
who never won anything, cantering in a field
then nuzzling your niece's hand
as she feeds him carrots or slices
of apple. Or it might be the light
that weaves through her hair—
touchable, untouchable light, the kind
that announces beauty and season
as it startles every strand
when she turns her head.
Sometimes it is even
words—single words thrown in
as if an afterthought, little gems
with their own kind of brilliance:
The horsey tickled in my hand, she said,
as she drifted into sleep and clenched
the memory. But mostly it is not
the words at all, but something unsaid,
something poems try to net
when we haul them into the dark
hours of morning when nothing yet
is spoken or lit. As now
between one word and the next

I remember the way her mother
breathed as she looked down at her
in that darkness as she slept, or,
actually, the way her mother's breath
leapt for a moment, as if she could find nothing
at all this fine and would take nothing less.

POEM FOR MY BROTHER, MANAGER OF A GO-GO BAR IN ROSELLE PARK, NEW JERSEY

Some night between midnight and three
when the last of the great pinchers
has finished his final drink
and you have taken his keys
and walked him out to the slick
New Jersey street, wet with the glaze
of approaching morning, and told him
to sleep it off in his own back seat,
then walked slowly back to the bar,
picking up debris and trash, tidying
the sidewalk, thinking about tomorrow,
about the girls who don't mean anything
or the greasy spot on the pavement
that is always there, no matter what
the weather, the streetlight out front
the only moon you ever see—
before you step inside and tend
the last of the sweeping and breathe
the last of the evening's smoke,
the music turned down but still on
so you won't be lonely, it would be sweet
if you would remember me, your only sister
ten years older and distant in miles

and habit, living for fifteen years
in the backwoods of a southern state
you've never seen, in a dry county
(where there still are such things)
rubbing the backs of her achy legs
with alcohol to suffocate
the chiggers, as she sits at the edge
of her homemade deck facing east
and thinks of you, as someone might
leaf through a history book and glance
at the pictures of places she has been,
or bends over a child's telescope
taking turns with her son and husband,
and names planets at a glimpse.
Tonight the music here is calm as crickets
and in a minute it is all I'll hear
as I put my son to bed and step out
again to watch the dark grow black
as the moon recedes, while somewhere east
the moon's already tipped her hat and you
have latched the latch and put the keys
in your pocket, whistling, clicking
down the street to your car, glancing back,
thinking that this is the only life
you'd ever wished for or dreamed.

ADVICE

First,
you've mistaken the crazy
for the mysterious. Strange-eyed
women with layers of feathers
or lace are not necessarily
hiding something.
If you must, search only
in the dark. Pick flowers.
Peel fruit. Dust.

Or look for a woman who hides
nothing. Look hard.
More than likely she's the one.
There is, of course, a price.
For a poem or two
she'll open her scars.
She'll sing to you all night
in the foreign tongue
of her womb. She'll fly.

Or look at that mirror.
The clue that lures you
lies between the glass and
the silver, between the shadow
and the ice. Do not move.
Open your eyes.

SNOW WHITE

It was actually one of the dwarfs
who kissed her—Bashful,
who still won't admit it.
That is why she remained in the forest
with all of them and made up
the story of the prince. Otherwise,
wouldn't you be out there now
scavenging through wildflowers,
mistaking the footprints of your own
children for those little men?
And if you found some wild apples
growing in the thickest part, if no one
were looking, wouldn't you
take a bite? And pray
some kind of magic sleep
would snatch you
from the plainness
of your life?

THIS IS AN ANSWER

We don't know what is asked.
We take long walks, leap

fences in stride, our heads down,
looking for it. We don't know

anything about it. We walk.
We take nothing with us but this

emptiness. Hands in our pockets,
we cross bridges that have already

knelt into rivers. We do not notice
what men have made, but there are clues

in what they have not. Something calls
from deep in the meadow. Even now

a place is being prepared.
A cloud glows,

then grows dark and restless.
Under the grass a worm moves out

of its skin. Even the largest stones
in the brook are turning to water.

TRYING TO EXPLAIN

Do you ask someone why he grows his fingernails?
—Robert Bly

I. The Field

In a burned field
I find the white shell
of a turtle. Pale bone
on this black lake of death,
it seems to float with purpose,
lone swan looking for its mate.

My own deep shell moves within
its soft house with ease,
as if flesh could prevent
what the mind agrees is true
but refuses to believe.
In my pocket
the turtle's song rests,
but in my head the grievous sound
moves on in long monotony
like those long-ago voices
at my mother's wake
whose dirge returned again and again,
long after the ground had received her,
sweet pocket in the earth,
which for me still breathes.

II. The Beach

Late in the day I find a translucent shell
on a beach no one visits much—
the houses of the city have moved
toward the shore: too many houses
where there should be only nests.
It is a dry abandoned shell, a house
without a dreamer, and I,
who dream all the time
and remember so little, do not
put it back.

III. The Woods

Toward evening a woodpecker tolls
the death of an oak. A star
winks through the early shadows.
From deep in my blood the ink
is already rising. There is a hawk
who is crazy for me all night.
Already I hear him calling. Already
I have begun the long hard climb
to meet him.

THIS

is the bread I make
and the bed I lie awake in.

It is the curtain
I pull to one side

when I want the stars
for friends. It is

the coin I spend
and the laundry

I wash over and over.
It is the rain I watch

and which I want
never to end.

There are times I wish
I could invite you,

and say, *Taste this*
or say, *Try your head here.*

But you have other places
to go. And this

is my place,
my travelling companion,

my one-woman show.

DAWN

This is the name
for the moment the quiet house
shifts between night and morning.

I sit in my swivel chair
in a room with two views, waiting
to catch it, the very moment.

Behind me the moon moves slowly down.
Before me the sky lightens, and
tree sounds change from frog

to bird. At first
the sun is an orange line
along the housetops.

Then it is a white ball,
and the moon
is gone.

This happens so fast
I've come dawn after dawn
to slow it down, to trap it.

I want to know what it is.
Not scientifically,
but with my whole body.

I want to know the precise moment
today became yesterday;
tomorrow, today. I want to say

I've gone deep enough,
that I've borrowed nothing, that
I've waited. But this is difficult.

I need to know so urgently exactly how
the woman who lies awake at night
becomes the sleeper, then the dreamer,

then the dream. I want to know why
the words I am saying seem to be spoken
by somebody else.

The sun is higher than my window now
and out of sight.
It is still winter.

I have to know what it's like
the moment that ice is not ice anymore
but isn't yet water.